# Rebuilding th Reconstruction Era Cartoons and Other Illustrations 1863 – 1877

Edited by

*Catherine McGrew Jaime*

**Non-fiction works by Catherine Jaime include:**
*Booker T. Washington and W.E.B. DuBois:*
      *Two Speeches and an Essay* (Annotated and Illustrated)

*Tales from the Troubled South: Civil Rights in Alabama*
*The Rocky Road to Civil Rights in the United States*
      (an annotated timeline)
*Da Vinci: His Life and His Legacy*
*Sharing Shakespeare with Students*
*Understanding (and Teaching) the United States Constitution*

**Historical fiction books by Catherine Jaime include:**
*York Proceeded On: The Lewis and Clark Expedition*
      *Through the Eyes of Their Forgotten Member*
*The Attack Trilogy*
*Failure in Philadelphia?*
*Leonardo the Florentine*
*Leonardo: Masterpieces in Milan*

Photographs and drawings used in this work are all in the public domain or used with permission.

Creative Learning Connection
8006 Old Madison Pike, Ste 11-A
Madison, AL 35758
www.CreativeLearningConnection.com

# Illustrations

# Introduction

During the first twelve years after the Civil War the United States was involved in its "Reconstruction" efforts. Out of that era came three amendments to the U.S. Constitution, a Freedmen's Bureau that came and went, and a variety of Civil Rights bills.

This project started as a look at many of the important documents from the Reconstruction Era. But this portion of it soon took on a life of its own – focusing on dozens of illustrations, primarily political cartoons, many of them from Thomas Nast's work during this era. Thomas Nast, "Father of the American Cartoon," was especially well known for his political cartoons during this era and beyond.

A note of warning about Nast's cartoons – they can be a bit "in your face." It is important to keep in mind the time period that he drew these in, and the messages he was trying to convey. Some of his cartoons appear more like racial caricatures, but as a general rule, he was extremely pro-minorities, and used his incredible drawing ability to focus on difficult issues of his day. His political cartoons, like the other drawings that I have chosen to include here, are generally full of complex messages. Please do not dismiss these works too quickly.

The cartoons and other illustrations are arranged chronologically. By themselves they make an interesting pictorial look at the Reconstruction Era, or they could be combined with any number of the related documents from that time period.

*Slaves Being Driven South by the Rebel Officers*
Illustration in *Harper's Weekly*, February 1862, Artist Unknown

*Harper's Weekly was a political magazine published from 1857 until 1917, and based in New York City. Illustrations such as these were an important part of Harper's Weekly's message during and after the Civil War.*

*Abe Lincoln's Last Card*
Cartoon by Englishman John Tenniel, 1862
referring to Lincoln's Emancipation Proclamation

*A Negro Regiment in Action*
Thomas Nast illustration in *Harper's Weekly*, March 1863

*Thomas Nast was a featured illustrator for Harper's Weekly for more than twenty years. Most of the cartoons used in this book were drawn by Nast for Harper's Weekly.*

*First Reading of the Proclamation*
Painting by Francis Bicknell Carpenter, 1864

*Man reading a newspaper with headline*
*"Presidential Proclamation, Slavery"*
Painting by Henry Louis Stephens, c.1863

*Celebrating Emancipation*
Thomas Nast illustration in *Harper's Weekly*, 1865

*Compromise with the South:*
*Dedicated to the Chicago Convention*
Thomas Nast illustration in *Harper's Weekly,* September 1864

*In 1864 the Democratic National Convention was held in Chicago to nominate their party's presidential candidate. The party was split between War Democrats and Peace Democrats. The party nominated a War Democrat, General George B. McClellan, but adopted a peace platform.*

## The "Rail Splitter" at Work Repairing the Union
### Illustration by Joseph E. Baker

*This 1865 cartoon shows President Abraham Lincoln with his Vice-President, Andrew Johnson. Lincoln commends Johnson, "A few more stitches Andy and the good old Union will be mended." Johnson warns, "Take it quietly Uncle Abe and I will draw it closer than ever."*

*President Lincoln Entering Richmond*
Thomas Nast cartoon, April 1865

*This Thomas Nast cartoon shows President Lincoln being greeted by emancipated slaves as he enters Richmond, Virginia.*

*Office of the Freedmen's Bureau, Memphis, Tennessee*
Illustration from *Harper's Weekly* by an unknown artist

*Juneteenth Celebration in Texas in 1900*
*(thirty-five years after the original "Juneteenth" of 1865).*

*On June 19, 1865 Texans received word of the abolition of slavery throughout the former Confederate states.*

*"Shall I trust these men, and not this man?"*
Thomas Nast illustration in *Harper's Weekly,* 1865

*Columbia (a personification of the U.S.A.) considering why she should pardon Confederate troops when an African American Union soldier with an amputated leg does not have the right to vote.*

*The Freedmen's Bureau*
A.R. Waud illustration in *Harper's Weekly,* June 1868

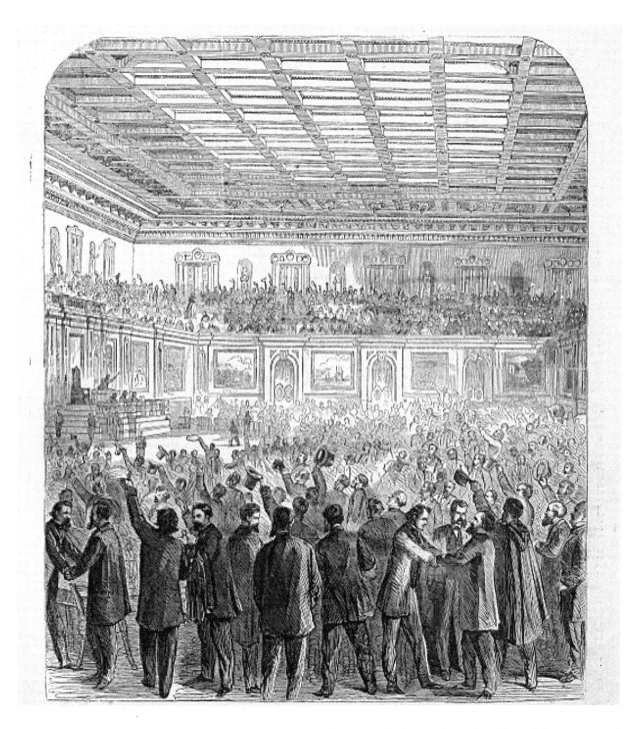

*Harper's Weekly cartoon depicting celebration in the House of Representatives after adoption of the Thirteenth Amendment.*

*US President Andrew Johnson Disbanding the Freedmen's Bureau*
Thomas Nast illustration, April 1866.

*Celebration of the Abolition of Slavery
in the District of Columbia by the Colored People,
in Washington, April 19, 1866*
Frederick Dielman illustration in *Harper's Weekly*, May 1866

*Slavery is Dead?*
*"The Land of the Free. State Rights. The Home of the Brave."*
Thomas Nast illustration, 1866

*Memphis Race Riots, May 1866*
*Scenes in Memphis, Tennessee, During the Riot – Shooting Down*
*Negroes on the Morning of May 2, 1866.*
Alfred Rudolph Waud illustration in *Harper's Weekly*

*The Riot in New Orleans, July 1866*
Left: *Murdering Negros in the Rear of Mechanics Institute*
Right: *Platform in Mechanics Institute After the Riot.*
Theodore R. Davis illustration in Harper's Weekly

*Johnson – President or King?*

Thomas Nast illustration in *Harpers' Weekly,* November 1866

*Freedmen Voting in New Orleans, 1867*

*In spite of Johnson's claims that the vast majority of Negroes had neither asked for nor wanted the right to vote, as this engraving shows, freedmen were very quick to sign up to vote when given the opportunity.*

*The Georgetown Elections - the Negro at the Ballot-box*
Thomas Nast illustration in *Harpers' Weekly*, March 1867

*Southern justice and the president's veto
of the military government bill*
Thomas Nast illustration in *Harper's Weekly*, March 1867

*A statue of a snake-haired man wearing a toga with a CSA belt
holding a scale tipping in favor of the South; the unjust results of
trials involving southerners and northerners; and depictions of
atrocities committed against African Americans.*

*"We Accept the Situation"*
Thomas Nast illustration in *Harper's Weekly*, April 1867

*An African American, former Union soldier, happily displays his "A Vote" paper while a former Confederate soldier stands near his paper declaring "No vote." Behind him is sign reading "Except such as may be disfranchised [sic] for participation in the Rebellion or for felony".*

*Significant Election Scene at Washington*
A.W. M'Callum illustration in *Harper's Weekly,* June 1867

*Seated men look on while other blacks and whites prepare to place their ballots into the election box.*

*The First Vote*
A. R. Waud illustration on the cover of *Harper's Weekly*, 1867

*A series of African American men await their chance to vote for the first time – representing a laborer, a businessman, a soldier, and a farmer.*

*The Union as it Was*
Subtitle: *The Lost Cause, Worse than Slavery*
Thomas Nash illustration in *Harper's Weekly*, 1867 or 1874?

*Nast depicts a man representing the "White League" shaking hands with a Ku Klux Klan member. Between them is a shield depicting an African American family cowering under the words "Worse than Slavery." In the background a man is shown hanging from a tree.*

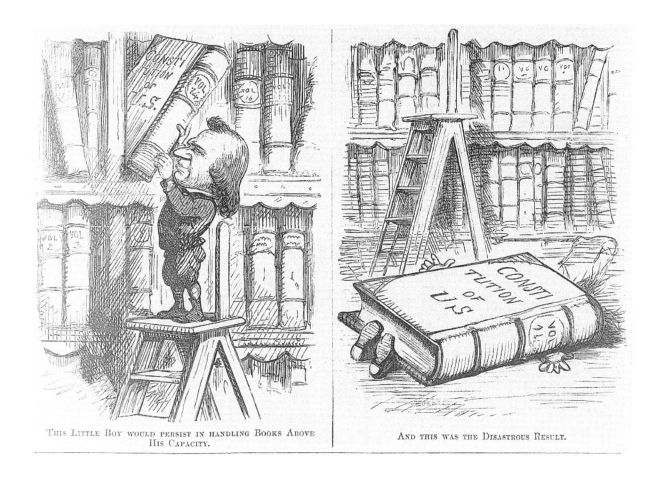

THIS LITTLE BOY WOULD PERSIST IN HANDLING BOOKS ABOVE HIS CAPACITY.

AND THIS WAS THE DISASTROUS RESULT.

*This little boy would persist in handling books above his capacity. And this was the disastrous result.*
Cartoon is unsigned, but is attributed to Thomas Nast.
Illustration in *Harper's Weekly,* March 1868

*Cartoon depicts Andrew Johnson standing on the top step of a step-ladder and lifting a large, heavy book from a high bookshelf; he falls off the ladder and is crushed by the book, the "Constitution of U.S."*

*The Senate as a Court of Impeachment
for the Trial of President Johnson, 1868*
Theodore R. Davis sketch in *Harper's Weekly*, April 1868.

*A ticket to be admitted to the Senate gallery
during Johnson's impeachment trial.*

*The Situation*
Illustration in *Harper's Weekly*, March 1868

*Shows Secretary of War Stanton aiming a cannon labeled "Congress" to defeat President Johnson. The rammer is "Tenure of Office Bill" and cannonballs on the floor are "Justice."*

Title: *"This is a white man's government"*
Subtitle: *"We regard the Reconstruction Acts (so called) of Congress as usurpations, and unconstitutional, revolutionary, and void"* - Democratic Platform
Thomas Nast illustration in *Harper's Weekly,* September 1868

*Cartoon showing man with belt buckle "CSA" holding a knife "the lost cause," a stereotyped Irishman holding club "a vote," and another man wearing a button "5 Avenue" and holding wallet "capital for votes," with their feet on an African American soldier sprawled on the ground. In the background, a "colored orphan asylum" and a "southern school" are in flames; African American children have been lynched near the burning buildings.*

*The National Colored Convention in Session at Washington, D.C.*
Theodore R. Davis illustration in *Harper's Weekly,* February 1869

*In 1869 the "Colored" National Labor Union was founded in Washington, D.C. by an assembly of more than two hundred African American artisans, engineers, mechanics, tradesmen and trades-women, and their supporters. The labor union pursued equal representation in the workforce for African Americans.*

*The Cincinnati Convention, in a Pickwickian Sense*
Subtitle: *"Men and Brethren! A new leaf must be turned over, or there are breakers ahead. The Cincinnati Convention may prove a fiasco, or it may name the next President."*
Illustration by Thomas Nast in *Harper's Weekly*, April 1872

*Nast mocks the upcoming Liberal Republican Convention that was to occur the following month in Cincinnati, with this parody of Charles' Dickens' novel,* The Pickwick Papers.

*Mud on the White House*
Thomas Nast in *Harper's Weekly*, May 4, 1872

### *Columbia*.

"O judgment, thou art fled to brutish beasts,
And men have lost their reason!
They, that have done this deed, are honorable;
What private griefs they have, alas, I know not,
That made them do it; they are wise and honorable,
And will, no doubt, with reasons answer you.
I come not, friends, to steal away your hearts;
I am no orator, as Brutus is:
I tell you that which you yourselves do know."
— Julius Caesar, Act III, Scene II.

*Lady Columbia points indignantly to some mud stains on the columns of the White House and delivers a lecture taken from Shakespeare's Julius Caesar.*

*The First Colored Senator and Representatives*
*in the 41$^{st}$ and 42$^{nd}$ Congress of the United States*
Currier & Ives Lithograph, 1872

*From left to right: Mississippi Senator Hiram Revels, Alabama Representative Benjamin Turner, South Carolina Representative Robert DeLarge, Florida Representative Josiah Walls, Georgia Representative Jefferson Long, and South Carolina Representatives Joseph Rainey and Robert B. Elliot.*

"Halt!"

Subtitle: *"This is not the way to 'repress corruption and to initiate the Negroes into the ways of honest and orderly government.'"*
Thomas Nast illustration in *Harper's Weekly*, October 1874

*Justice swings the sword of Law into the White Men's League as they stand on the body of an African American man they appear to have killed.*

*The Shackle Broken – By the Genius of Freedom, 1874*
by E. Sachse and Company

*Central illustration shows South Carolina Representative Robert B. Elliott delivering a speech in favor of the Civil Rights Act. Other images are scenes of African-American soldiers in the Civil War, a farm and statues of President Abraham Lincoln and Senator Charles Sumner. Extracts from Elliot's speech appear throughout the cartoon.*

*Shall we Call Home our Troops?*
Subtitle: *"We intend to beat the negro in the battle of life & defeat means one thing – EXTERMINATION"* - Birmingham (Alabama) News
Illustration in *Harper's Weekly*, January 1875

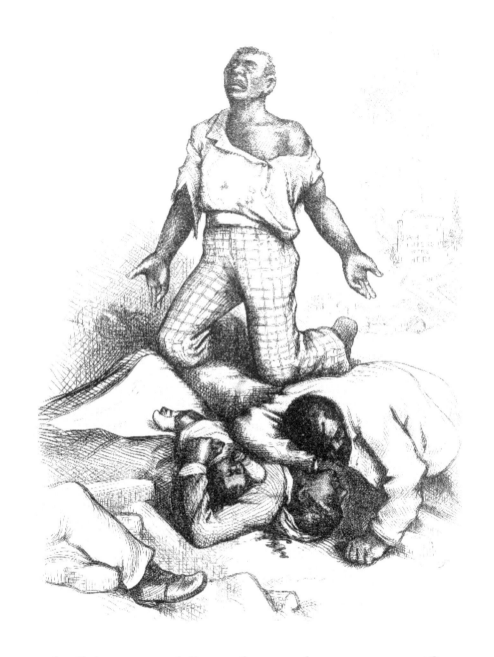

*Is this a republican form of government?*
Subtitle: *Is this protecting life, liberty, or property?*
*Is this the equal protection of the laws?*
Thomas Nast illustration in *Harper's Weekly*, September 1876

*In the background a barely visible sign reads "The White Liners Were Here."*

*Thomas Nast's 1870 cartoon depicting the Democratic party as a Donkey, from Harper's Weekly.*

*Thomas Nast's 1874 cartoon depicting the Republicans as an Elephant. It also appeared in Harper's Weekly.*

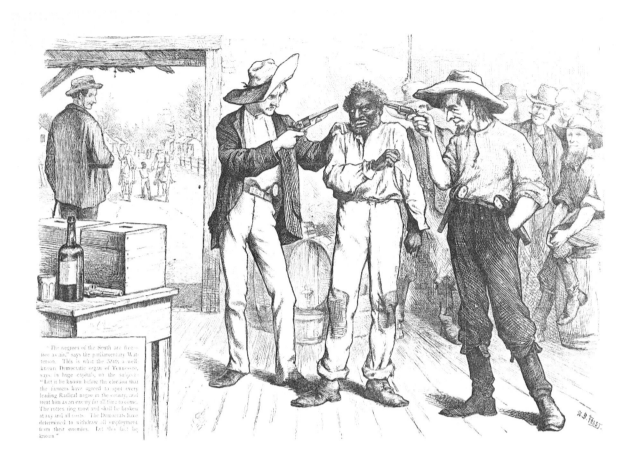

*"Of Course He Wants to Vote the Democratic Ticket"*
Subtitle: *"You're as free as air, ain't you?*
*Say you are, or I'll blow yer black head off!"*
Arthur Burdett Frost illustration in *Harper's Weekly*, October 1876

*A note in the corner of the cartoon reads, "The negroes of the South are free – free as air" says the parliamentary Watterson. This is what the State, a well known Democratic organ of Tennessee, says in huge capitals, on the subject: 'Let it be known before the election that the farmers have agreed to spot every leading Radical negro in the country, and treat him as an enemy for all time to come. The rotten ring must and shall be broken at any and all costs. The Democrats have determined to withdraw all employment from their enemies. Let this fact be known.'"*

*The Color Line is Broken*
Thomas Nast illustration in *Harper's Weekly*, December 1877

*Death at the polls, and free from "Federal Interference"*
Thomas Nast illustration in *Harper's Weekly*, October 1879

*The skeleton wears a "Solid Southern Shot Gun" belt as he prevents African Americans from voting.*

*What Does the Colored Race Have to be Thankful for?*
Thomas Nast illustration in *Harper's Weekly,* November 1886